MILK
FOR NEW CHRISTIANS

Frank Hamrick & Jerry Dean

PositiveAction
BIBLE CURRICULUM

Milk: For New Christians

Copyright 1972, 2005, 2008 by Positive Action For Christ, Inc., P.O. Box 700, 502 W. Pippen St., Whitakers, NC 27891. All rights reserved. No part may be reproduced in any manner without permission in writing from the publisher.

Quotations are from the King James Version of the Bible.

First edition published 1972
Second edition published 2005
Third edition published 2008

Printed in the United States of America

ISBN: 1-929784-48-1

Designed by Shannon Brown
Cover Artwork by Chris Ellison

Published by

TABLE OF CONTENTS

As newborn babes, desire the sincere milk of the word, that ye may grow thereby.
(1 Pet. 2:2)

Do you want to mature and be all that God wants you to be? Are you willing to seek the blessings the Lord has for you? Do you want to know your God better and be able to glorify Him with your life? If you really mean business, this booklet is for you. It will provide you with the milk you need to get started in the right direction.

Stop now unless you are determined to finish. If you're ready to begin, pray and ask God to open your heart that you may be able to understand His Word and apply its teachings to your life "that ye may grow thereby."

1

HOW DO I BECOME A CHRISTIAN?

The Bible speaks much about "salvation." But what does this really mean?

In the natural world, we may think of it as saving a person from physical death or harm. However, when the Bible uses the word, it is speaking in reference to something far more important than even physical death!

Biblical salvation refers to two main things: 1) one's rescue from eternal separation from God in the lake of fire and 2) a renewal of one's ability to enjoy God forever, both on this earth and in the world to come!

When a person is "saved" he is called a "Christian." It is therefore of paramount importance that we know how to become a Christian.

Works Don't Save

Maybe you're asking, "Don't I have to do something to get saved? Aren't good works necessary to get me to heaven?"

What does God's Word say? Turn to Romans 3:9–12.

- Verse 9 teaches that both Jew and Gentile are the same in that they are both under _Sin_.

- What does this mean? _We are all Sinners no matter who it is_

- Verse 10 shows what we really are in the sight of God. How many are righteous (right with God)? _No one is righteous_

- According to verse 11, how many people really seek God? _None_

- How many people, according to verse 12, do good in God's sight? _Not one_

What about this question? Can an unsaved person do good!

- So far as pleasing mankind, any of us can do good!

- So far as pleasing God, no lost person can do good! Romans 8:8 says that those who are in the flesh (that is, those who are still unsaved) _Cannot_ please God.

So far as salvation is concerned, no one can please God!

God Is Holy

Read Leviticus 11:44 and answer the following questions.

- What did God require of Israel?
  that they sandify Themselves

- Why must they be holy?
  Because God is holy

- Read Habakkuk 1:13. God is so holy that He cannot _look on iniquity_.

God is perfectly holy and He demands holiness from every individual.

- Romans 3:23 tells us we are _All_ sinners.

- Can a person who is sinful (unholy) please a perfectly holy God by his own works? ☐ Yes ☒ No.

As we shall see, God is so holy that even our good works appear to Him as sinful.

Because God is holy, our sins separate us from Him.

- What does Romans 6:23 tell us are the wages for our sin?
  Death

Salvation Is a Gift

- According to Romans 6:23, how does a person get eternal life?
  through Jesus our Lord

- What does a person have to do to get a gift?
  receive it

- If a person offers you a gift, do you tell them, "Well, that's great, but let me pay for it and earn it"?
  ☐ Yes ☒ No

- Is there any way you can work for a free gift?
  ☐ Yes ☒ No

If you work for a gift, it is no longer a gift. It's a wage! Note this verse again. Salvation is a gift from God to us through the Lord Jesus Christ. All we can do is accept that gift.

Our Righteousnesses Are Worthless

- What does Isaiah 64:6 tell us about our righteousnesses (good works)?
  They are as filthy rags

The phrase, *filthy rags* (or *polluted garments*), is a term which actually refers to bandages that cover an open sore. Have you ever wrapped an open sore with gauze and later removed the gauze? It's a terrible sight, isn't it? That gauze is what God says our attempts to please Him are like!

When/How Does a Person Become a Christian?

A person becomes a Christian when the following things happen.

He Recognizes That He Is a Condemned Sinner before a Holy God

In John 4 Christ confronted the woman of Sychar with her sinfulness by reminding her of her five marriages. How did the following admit their sinfulness?

- David—2 Samuel 12:13
  Said he had sinned

- Isaiah 6:5
  Said he was a man of unclean lips

He Discovers What Christ Has Done for Him

In Acts 8, the Ethiopian Eunuch wondered how to be saved. Philip used Isaiah 53 to explain to him that Christ died for his sins. Salvation would not be possible had Christ not paid for our sins on the cross. (See 1 Pet. 1:17-18; Rom. 5:6). Without an understanding of Christ's saving work on the cross, a man cannot be saved.

God's holiness and justice demand death for our sins (Rom. 6:23). The good news is that Christ died in our place!

He Repents of His Sin and Flees to Christ for Salvation

- What does 2 Corinthians 7: 10 tell us that godly sorrow produces? __worketh repentance__ What does this lead to? __Salvation__

Repentance means to make an about face, to change one's mind and direction.

- How does a man get repentance (2 Tim. 2:25)?
  __acknowledging truth__

There are two kinds of repentance: Man's repentance and God-given repentance. One saves; the other does not! How do we know that our repentance is saving repentance? There are two signs that accompany God-given (saving) repentance.

1. We will have godly __repentance__ for our sin (2 Cor. 7:10). This is an actual hatred of our sin and a deep desire to be cleansed of it.

2. We will see that Christ is more __precious__ _____ (valuable, treasured, priceless) than all else in this world (1 Pet. 2:7), and we will desire Him.

- Read Matthew 13:44. How did the man act who found the treasure in the field?
  __hides it then does what it takes to acquire it__

(The treasure represents Christ. When a man truly repents of his sin, he realizes that Christ is more valuable and more to be desired than all the treasures on earth. He will do anything to gain that glorious treasure.)

He Believes on the Lord Jesus Christ with All His Heart

- Read John 3:16. According to this verse, who will be given eternal life?

  Whosoever believeth in Him

Salvation is more than a simple business transaction in which God offers to save us if we will believe and we say, "Okay, I believe." Like repentance, there is also a belief that does not save and a belief that does save.

- James 2:19 tells us that the _devils_ believe that there is only one God. Obviously, this belief does not save!

The kind of belief Jesus spoke of to Nicodemus (John 3:16) is saving belief. How is it different from the belief that the demons have? Saving belief is born from a clear conviction of God's holiness, our sinfulness, and our utter helplessness to save ourselves. It continues with a realization of the preciousness of Christ, who alone can save, culminating in our desperate trust in what He did on the cross to save us from our sins.

Complete This Section without Looking Back at the Lesson

1. How many people have sinned? _all_

2. What are the wages for our sins? _death_

3. Can unsaved people do anything right and pleasing to God? ☐ Yes ☒ No

4. Can unsaved people do good deeds in the sight of other men? ☒ Yes ☐ No

5. According to Romans 6:23, is eternal life (salvation) earned by man, or is it a gift of God? _gift_

6. In God's sight how do man's righteousnesses (his attempts to earn salvation) appear? _as_
   filthy rags

7. What is the only thing a man can do to get saved?
   believe on Christ + repent

8. What are the 4 things that take place when a man is truly saved?
   given eternal life
   filled w the Holy Spirit
   sins are forgiven
   become children of God
   washed us white as snow

God commands us to hide His Word in our hearts. The best way to do that is to memorize it.

Learn the following verses. They will remind you that salvation is a free gift to all who will believe on Jesus Christ and depend on Him alone to save them.

Verses to Memorize

- Ephesians 2:8, 9

2
THE ASSURANCE
OF SALVATION

Can a person know whether or not he is saved? There are those who teach that we can only hope we will go to heaven when we die. Some go so far as to teach that even the Apostle Paul was not certain he was saved! But Scriptures clearly teach that we can know whether or not we are saved. In fact, one whole book in the Bible was written that we might know whether or not God has saved us (1 John).

Study the following ways we can know whether or not we are saved.

Christ's Life Assures

When God saves a person, something happens to him on the inside.

The Old Sinner Dies

- Read Galatians 2:20. What happens to a person whom God saves (first phrase)?

  _____

  _____

God Places a New Life Within

- According to Galatians 2:20 what (Who) is this new life that lives within a believer?

  _____

- According to Colossians 3:4, what (Who) is this new life that now lives inside a new Christian?

  _____

- How does Galatians 2:20 explain this?

  _____

  _____

  _____

This New Life (Christ) Cannot Die

Psalm 110 is a psalm about Christ, written 1000 years before He was born! It describes Him in several ways. One picture it uses if that of Melchizedek, an ancient King-Priest in Jerusalem. He is described in Hebrews 6:3 as living forever. In this way he was a picture (type) of Christ, who lives forever.

- What phrase in this psalm says that Christ is a priest that will never die?

  _____

  _____

- According to Revelation 11:15, how long will Christ endure?_____

Since the eternal Christ lives in a believer and is his very life, the believer is assured that he will forever be saved.

But, what if Christ leaves a believer?

Christ Will Never Leave the New Believer

- Read Hebrews 13:5. What will Christ never do?

  _____

Those Who Have Christ Have Eternal Life

Read 1 John 5:11–13 and answer the following questions.

- Who gives eternal life? _____
- Does everyone possess eternal life? ☐ Yes ☐ No
- Who does possess eternal life? _____
- Where is eternal life? _____

  _____

- Who does not have eternal life? _____
  _____

- To whom were these verses written? _____

- According to these verses, can you really know you have eternal life? ☐ Yes ☐ No

- How can you know you have eternal life?
  _____
  _____
  _____

Since Christ (who will never die) lives in believers and since He has promised to never leave them, then believers can never go to hell. Christ's life assures us of eternal salvation!

God's Word Assures

Read Acts 16:30, 31; Romans 10:9, 13; John 3:16. Now answer the following questions.

- In your own words, what must a person do to be saved?
  _____
  _____
  _____

- Can God lie (Titus 1:2)? ☐ Yes ☐ No

- Did God say He would save you if you put your faith and trust in Him? ☐ Yes ☐ No

- Are you trusting Him for salvation? ☐ Yes ☐ No

- According to God's Word, then, are you saved?
  ☐ Yes ☐ No

God's Hands Assure

Read John 10:27–29. These verses show that we, as believers, are in Christ's hand (vs. 28) and in God the Father's hand (vs. 29).

- Can anyone take us out of these hands? ☐ Yes   ☐ No

- Study verse 28. *Perish* in this verse means to suffer in hell. If a person is God's child, in His hands, will he ever perish? ☐ Yes   ☐ No

- What phrase in John 10:28 proves this?

  _____

  _____

- Do you think it is up to you to keep yourself saved?
  ☐ Yes   ☐ No

- Look at 1 Peter 1:5. According to this verse, what guards us through faith unto salvation?

  _____

  _____

Dealing with Doubts

It is obvious that the devil will try to convince you that you are not really saved. Perhaps you have already had some doubts. Don't worry. It is common for people to doubt that God would want to save them.

Well, I Just Don't Feel Saved!

Read John 1:12 and complete the following statement.

- God gives to those who receive Jesus Christ the power to

  _____ .

- According to this verse, what have you become by receiving Christ?_____

- Do you have to *feel* like you are the child of your parents to really be their child? ☐ Yes   ☐ No

- Some mornings you may get out of bed and not even feel alive! Does that mean you are not living?
☐ Yes   ☐ No

- Is it a fact or a feeling that you are now a child of God?
☐ Fact   ☐ Feeling

Complete This Section without Looking Back at the Lesson

1. How does Christ's life give us assurance that we are eternally saved?

   _____
   _____
   _____
   _____

2. Who possesses eternal life? _____

   _____

3. Do you possess eternal life? ☐ Yes   ☐ No

4. How do you know? _____

   _____
   _____

5. What verse of Scripture teaches that you can know you have eternal life?_____

6. In your own words, what does a person have to do to be saved? _____

   _____

_____

_____

7. What verses teach that you're in Christ's hands?

_____

8. First Peter 1:5 says you are kept by what?

_____

_____

9. List the three major proofs for the assurance of salvation.

_____

_____

_____

Verses to Memorize

- 1 John 5:13
- Romans 10:9

3

THE IMPORTANCE
OF GOD'S WORD

Now that you know you're born again, that you have become a new creature (2 Cor. 5:17), you may ask, "What do I do now? There's got to be more to it than this!" You're right. There is more—lots more. A normal, loving parent would not leave a newborn infant to take care of himself; neither does God leave a newborn Christian to grow for himself. But how do you grow as a Christian?

The Word of God is the means by which you can grow and become a stronger Christian (1 Pet. 2:2). It makes sense that the more you read about someone, the more you will know about that person. God is the author of the Bible. As you read His Word, you will learn more about Him and how you should live that He might be glorified.

What God Says about His Word

- According to Psalm 138:2, what has God done to His Word? _____

  _____

- Why did Christ say He had come to earth in Matthew 5:17–18? _____

- According to the same passage, how much of God's Word is true (will be fulfilled)?_____

- What did Christ say about the authority of His own words in Matthew 24:35?_____

  _____

- According to 2 Timothy 3:16, what is true about all Scripture? _____

  _____

- What did Christ say about the authority of the Scriptures in John 10:35? _____

  _____

- Can a person be born again (saved) apart from the Word of God? ☐ Yes ☐ No

- What is the Old Testament about according to John 5:39? _____

_____

Answer the following questions from 1 Peter 1:23.

- How is a person born again? _____

_____

- How long will God's Word be true?_____

- What does the Bible mean when it says that the Word of God is "incorruptible" or "imperishable"?

_____

_____

Note the following verses about the purpose of the Bible.

- How does a person get the faith to trust Christ (Rom. 10:17)?_____

_____

- Why was the Gospel of John written (John 20:31)?

_____

_____

Seven Results of Studying the Word of God

Look up the following verses about studying God's Word and match them with the results they bring by placing the correct letter in the blank provided.

Studying God's Word Will Help Me...

	1. Keep from sin	A. Psalm 119:116
	2. Build up (grow) spiritually	B. Psalm 119:105
	3. Live and not be ashamed	C. Psalm 119:99
	4. Know the truth	D. Psalm 119:11
	5. Know where I'm going	E. Hebrews 5:14
	6. Have understanding	F. Acts 20:32
	7. Know right from wrong	G. Psalm 119:160

How Should I Treat Something So Important?

You Should Do Seven Things with God's Word

Look up the passages given and state how you should treat God's
Word.

- Revelation 1:3 _____

  _____

- Acts 24:14 _____

  _____

- Revelation 22:7; James 1:22_____

  _____

- 2 Timothy 2:15 _____

  _____

- Psalm 119:11 _____

  _____

- What is the best way to hide it? _____

_____

- 1 Timothy 4:15 _____

_____

  - Define *meditate.* _____

  _____

- Philippians 2:16 _____

_____

Complete This Section without Looking Back at the Lesson

1. What is the only way a person can grow in the Lord?

    _____

2. Name seven things a study of the Word of God will do
    in your life.

    _____

    _____

    _____

    _____

    _____

    _____

    _____

3. What did Christ say about the authority of the
    Scriptures? _____

4. How does a person get the faith to trust Christ?

    _____

    _____

5. Why was God's Word written?

    _____

    _____

6. List three ways you should treat the Word of God. Include a Scripture reference with each.

_____

_____

_____

Verses to Memorize

- 2 Timothy 2:15
- 2 Timothy 3:16
- Psalm 119:9, 11

4

HOW TO STUDY
THE WORD

Would you look in a dictionary to find a phone number? Of course you wouldn't. In order to use the book effectively you must know its purpose. The same is true of the Bible. God wrote the Bible for a purpose, to reveal Himself to us. The key to reading the Bible is looking for God in every passage and verse you read.

The Word of God will also teach you about yourself. In James 1:22-25, the Word of God is compared to a mirror that shows us our innermost heart. As we look into this mirror, we are changed to become more like Christ.

Look for God in the Passage

God's Word was written primarily to reveal who He is. If we read it and don't see Him, we miss the whole point of Scripture.

- How did the scribes and Pharisees illustrate this idea in John 5:39? _____

    _____

- When you read the Word, take a sheet of paper and divide it into three sections as in the table below.

What God Does	Who God Is
How God Operates (Works)	

Under "What God Does," record everything you see God doing in the passage—even small things like walking, talking, and healing. Under "Who God Is," record attributes and characteristics this passage reveals about God (holiness, mercy, grace, justice, etc.). Under "How God Operates," record what you learn about the way God works (plans, concerned about my happiness, more interested in spiritual welfare than physical, etc.).

Make a copy of the preceding table on a separate shee of paper and fill it in using Mark 2:1-12.

Understand the "Story" of the Bible

The Bible is not a collection of stories that teach good moral truth. Rather, it is one story with one ultimate goal. Simply put, the Bible is the story of God's glory! The Bible begins with "God" (Gen. 1:1) and concludes with mention of God's grace (Rev. 22:21).

> **The Purpose of God's Word Is to Tell Us the Story of God's Glory and Grace.**

The Bible is God's self-revelation. It is His autobiography! As such, we should read it to learn His story and His glory. What is this story of His glory?

The Story of God's Glory

- God made man to glorify Him (Isa. 43:7 with Gen. 1-2).

- Satan wanted to steal God's glory, so he deceived Adam and Eve thereby blinding all men to God's glory (Gen. 3; 1 Cor. 4:4, 6).

- God, knowing this would happen, began an eternal plan to restore man's state so that he could once more see God's glory and enjoy Him. This plan we call God's "Plan of Redemption."

The Plan of Redemption

The history of God's Plan of Redemption is the sub-plot of the Story of God's Glory.

- God made a nation (Israel) from Abraham's seed. (Genesis)

- God prepared a land where that nation would live, Canaan, and brought those people to that land. (Exodus-Joshua)

- God selected the Davidic line of Abraham's seed through which a Redeemer would come. (1 Samuel)

- God protected and preserved that line, and eventually sent Jesus Christ through Mary, who was a direct descendant of David. (1 Samuel – Nehemiah)

- God used the prophets to reveal the coming of a future Messiah (Anointed One) who would redeem man. (Old Testament Prophets, Psalms)

- In the fullness of the time, the Messiah (Jesus Christ) was born of a virgin, died on the cross to pay for man's sin, and arose from the dead to save (redeem) men so they could once more see God's glory. (Matthew-John)

- Today, God is saving (redeeming, restoring, regenerating) a people to glorify His name (Acts 15:14) and sending them to proclaim His excellencies to the whole world (1 Pet. 2:9).

The Conclusion of the Story of God's Glory

All men will one day glorify God, bow to Christ as Lord, and give Him the glory. (Revelation, also see Phil. 2:11) Thus, God will ultimately fulfill the purpose for which He made man in the beginning.

It is imperative that you understand this story when you read the Bible. The Bible is not about David; it is about David's God. It is not about ancient heroes we should imitate. Rather it is about

God's great plan for His glory and our redemption. Every story you read, every chapter and book you study, and every exhortation you see in the Bible, fits inside that story. When you fail to see the passage in light of that story, you will miss the point of Scripture.

Discovering the Story of God's Glory

As a second exercise, take a sheet of paper and divide it into 4 equal sections labeled as follows.

God's Actions: (What God does in this passage)
His Glory: (What you learned about the character and attributes of God in this passage)
His Grace: (What you learned about God's grace, Christ, the cross, and the Gospel in this passage)
Other Thoughts: (Other things you may have learned or realized from this passage)

Read Genesis 1:1-8 and fill in the above sections as you read and meditate.

Looking into the Mirror of the Word

Read James 1:19-27 and answer the following questions.

- What should you be quick to do according to verse 19?

  _____

- But you shouldn't stop there. What two things should you be according to verse 22?

  _____

  _____

- What will happen if you do both of these things (vs. 25)?

  _____

  _____

- According to 2 Corinthians 3:18, what are the results of seeing God's glory in the Bible?

  _____

  _____

  _____

As you read God's Word, the Holy Spirit will convict you of ways you are falling short of God's glory. He will then use the Word to correct you and make you more like Christ. Thus as you respond to seeing God in the Word, you are being continually changed into His image.

Dependence on the Holy Spirit

Read 1 Corinthians 2:12-14 and answer the following questions.

- Who cannot understand God's Word? _____

- Who can understand God's Word?_____

- What is the only way a person can understand the Word?

  _____

  _____

Complete This Section without Looking Back at the Lesson

1. What is the key to Bible study? _____

   _____

2. What was God's purpose for creating man?

   _____

   _____

3. What is God doing today as part of the Plan of Redemption? _____

   _____

   _____

4. What are the results of seeing God's glory in the Bible?

_____

_____

_____

5. What is the only way a person can understand God's Word? _____

_____

6. Why can't unsaved people understand the Word?

_____

_____

_____

Verses to Memorize

- 1 Corinthians 2:14
- Psalm 119:97

5
PRAYER

You have learned that the Bible is God's Word; therefore, when you study it, the Lord is actually speaking to you. But in order to have complete fellowship with our Heavenly Father, you must also talk to Him each day. If you never spoke to your earthly father, what sort of relationship would you have? A very strained one at best! So, you must spend much time talking to the Lord, but there are some basic things you must first know about prayer.

Prayer and Sin

* The first thing to remember is that sin breaks fellowship with the Lord. Read Psalm 66:18 and state in your own words what this verse means. _____

_____

_____

_____

_____

How do you get rid of sin in your life? Do you have to be saved all over again? No! We've already learned that we have become sons of God and have eternal life. So what do you do if you sin? Read 1 John 1:9.

* What are we to do about sin?_____

_____

* What are the two things God will then do?

_____

_____

Note Nehemiah's prayer in Nehemiah 1:4–10.

* How did Nehemiah begin the prayer (vs. 5)?

_____

_____

- What did he do after these opening words of adoration (vs. 6, 7)? _____

- What did he claim in verses 8–10? _____

- What did he do in verse 11? _____

Nehemiah's prayer could be outlined as follows.

- Adoration and worship
- Confession of his sin
- Claiming God's promises
- Asking for help

- Most often we are only interested in doing one of the above. Which is it? _____

God will not answer prayer if sin is unconfessed!

Why We Can Pray

Study 1 Timothy 2:5 and 1 John 2:1. In these two passages the words *mediator* and *advocate* mean basically the same thing: Christ is literally your Lawyer. He pleads your case before God, showing Him that you are under His blood. When God looks at your sin, He sees only the righteousness of Christ. Christ actually deposited eternal life for you in the bank of heaven, signed His name to the deposit, and gave you the credit card. Because of His work, you can stand before God and speak to Him.

- Note Hebrews 10:19–22. With what attitude can you approach God in prayer? _____

- According to verse 19, what did Christ do that you might come boldly to the Father in prayer?

  _____

  _____

How to Pray

Read Ephesians 5:20; John 14:6, 13, 14; 15:16; 16:23, 26–27. Based on these verses, answer the following questions.

To Whom to Pray

- How does Jesus begin His prayer in Matthew 6:9?

  _____

  _____

- Should you pray to the Father, the Son, or the Holy Spirit?_____

- According to these verses, would it be best to pray, "Dear Jesus"? ☐ Yes ☐ No

In Whose Name to Pray

- What one phrase occurs over and over again in these verses? _____

  _____

- Whose name are these verses speaking of?

  _____

- Therefore, in whose name should we pray?

  _____

In Whose Power to Pray

When Christ went back into heaven, He promised to send the Comforter. Read John 14:16; 15:26; 16:7.

- Who is this Comforter? _____

- What does He do for you when you pray (Rom. 8:26)?

  _____

Definition of Prayer

Prayer is worship, addressed to the Father, in the name of the Son, in the power of the Holy Spirit.

How to Know Your Prayers Will Be Answered

There are certain prerequisites for answered prayer. Look up the following passages and write down the prerequisite in the space provided.

- 1 John 5:14–15 _____

  _____

- 1 Peter 3:12 _____

  _____

- Matthew 21:22 _____

  _____

- John 16:23 _____

  _____

- James 5:16–17 _____

  _____

Why God Answers Prayer

Why does God answer prayer according to the following verses?

- John 14:13 _____
  _____

- John 16:24 _____
  _____

For What to Pray

- There are six things we should pray for listed in Matthew 6:9–13. What are they?

  _____
  _____
  _____
  _____
  _____
  _____

Where and When to Pray

Based on Christ's example and teaching, what are the best time and place to meet the Lord each day (Mark 1:35; Matt. 6:5–6)?

- Time _____

- Place _____

Complete This Section without Looking Back at the Lesson

1. What one thing hinders answered prayer? _____

2. What should you always do before you ask God for anything? _____
   _____

3. Why is it possible to pray to God? _____
   _____

4. To whom should you pray, in whose name, and in whose power should you pray? _____

   _____

5. Why does God answer prayer? _____

   _____

6. What is prayer? _____

   _____

Verses to Memorize

- 1 Timothy 2:8
- Psalm 66:18
- 1 Peter 3:12

6

SHARING YOUR FAITH

You have probably often heard from your pastor and others about the importance of witnessing. But what exactly is a witness, and why is it important that you become one?

In a court case, a witness is someone who tells others about what he has seen or experienced, and in the Christian life, a witness does the same thing! He tells others about the glorious God who saved him and how they can know this same God.

Now that it is clear what a witness is, let's look at what should motivate us to want to share our faith.

Why Should a Christian Witness?

You Want the Whole World to See His Glory

Witnessing should be the natural result of our being so full of God and so zealous for His glory that we want the whole world to know.

- How did David express this (Ps. 71:24a)?

  _____

  _____

  _____

Read the following verses and state what ultimately drove Paul to be a missionary to the whole world.

- Romans 1:5

  _____

  _____

- 1 Corinthians 5:14

  _____

  _____

"For His name" means that Paul wanted everyone to know how wonderful, awesome, beautiful, and gracious, God is. Witnessing is nothing more than bragging about the God you love!

God Wants You to Witness

- What did Christ intend to make of every Christian (Matt. 4:19)? _____

- What should every saved person be (Acts 1:8)?

  _____

  _____

- What purpose was behind God making us His special people (1 Pet. 2:9)?

  _____

  _____

There Is No Other Way for Men to Be Won

- According to James 1:18 and 1 Peter 1:23, what is the instrument through which men are saved?

  _____

  _____

- According to Romans 10:14 what must happen before a man will trust Christ as his Lord and Savior?

  _____

  _____

- How does Romans 10:14 apply to your life? What is it challenging you to do?

  _____

  _____

Witnessing Is an Essential Means of Spiritual Growth

The more you declare the truth, the greater its hold on you. It increases faith and deepens love for Christ.

What If People Laugh at Me?

Why Some People Don't Witness

* Why do many professing Christians not witness (Pro. 29:25)? _____

  _____

* Why was Paul not ashamed to witness (Rom. 1:16)?

  _____

  _____

Paul was so excited about His God that he was compelled to witness! This should be the real reason we witness. When we don't witness, we reveal that we love other things more than the Lord.

Does It Matter How I Live?

Living Makes a Difference

The Christian should make sure he does not become a stumbling block. God's glory is preached not by words alone, but first of all by conduct. Words will be more effective if a person first sees what Christ can do in a life.

* Note Philippians 1:27. What was Paul's concern for the Philippian Christians?

  _____

  _____

- Note 1 Peter 2:11–15. From what is a Christian to abstain?

  _____

  _____

- What will the unsaved do when you have sin in your life (vs. 12)? _____

  _____

- How can you silence the criticisms of unsaved men (vs. 15)? _____

But I Don't Know What to Say!

How to Witness

It is essential to present four key truths to the unbeliever in the following order. After each reference given under the next four headings write out the phrase or phrases that teach the key truth.

God Is Holy, and the Unbeliever Is a Sinner

This is the first and most basic fact in witnessing. If a person doesn't see his need, in light of who God is, he will not seek a cure! Use the following verses to prove his sinfulness:

- Romans 3:10, 23

  _____

  _____

  _____

- Isaiah 53:6

  _____

  _____

  _____

Other Scriptures you may use include: Galatians 3:22, Jeremiah 17:9, and Ecclesiastes 7:20.

God Will Punish Man for His Sin

After the first point, the unbeliever may think, "So what? Yes, I am a sinner, but everyone else is a sinner as well. What's so bad about that?" Now show him the awful consequences of being a sinner.

Death

- Romans 6:23

  _____

  _____

  _____

- Ezekiel 18:4b

  _____

Hell and the Lake of Fire

- Luke 16:23

  _____

  _____

  _____

- Revelation 20:15

  _____

  _____

Christ Suffered Your Hell for You

Now comes the good news! After you have shown the person he is a sinner and under the condemnation of death and hell, you show him God's love and provision for his sin.

Christat Was Born to Save Men from Their Sin

- Matthew 1:21

  _____

  _____

  _____

  _____

He Came to Take away Our Sin

- John 1:29

  _____

  _____

  _____

  _____

He Bore Our Sins

- 1 Peter 2:24

  _____

  _____

  _____

  _____

He Died for the Ungodly

- Romans 5:6, 8

  _____

  _____

  _____

  _____

Here you should emphasize substitution to the unbeliever. Christ took our place on the cross! We are the ones condemned to die and suffer in hell, but because of His love for us, He came to earth and suffered our hell for us. God poured out His wrath on Christ as payment for our sin.

There Is Nothing Left to Do but Trust, or Believe

If Christ paid the debt on the cross, then man has nothing to pay. If you owe a debt and someone pays it for you, there is nothing left to do but accept it. Christ paid the debt for sin and now asks us to do the following.

Confess Him as the Lord (Boss) of Our Lives

*   Romans 10:9

     _____

     _____

     _____

Trust What He Did on the Cross to Provide Payment for Your Sin

*   John 3:16

     _____

     _____

     _____

Help! The Man Wants to Be Saved! What Do I Do Now?

Urge Him to Trust Christ as His Lord and Savior

Believers must be very careful at this point. Salvation is not the work of manipulation by men but is the work of regeneration by the Holy Spirit.

*   What did Paul tell the Philippian jailor in Acts 16:30-31?

     _____

     _____

*   In John 3:1-18, what did Jesus tell Nicodemus was necessary to be born again? _____

     _____

In both cases note what was *not* done. Neither was asked to repeat a special pray or do some other spiritual work.

- Note Acts 8:36-37. What did the man "do" for salvation?

_____

_____

It is not by prayer nor by following a formula that a man is saved. It is by simply *believing* (trusting) the simple truth that man is a sinner, that he cannot save himself, that Christ paid for his sin, and that by trusting in Him alone, he can go to heaven.

Be sure he understands that the only way of salvation is by trusting Christ and then, get out of the way! Salvation is a transformation in man that occurs when he accepts the gift of God. Be careful that you do not reduce it to a simple prayer or formula.

Help Him Grow

A new Christian is like a new baby (1 Pet. 2:2). He needs food and nourishment. He needs to grow. It is important that you follow up with a new believer by discipling him. One way to do this is to give him a copy this booklet and help him work through it. Another way is to get him into a strong Bible-teaching church.

Complete This Section without Looking Back at the Lesson

1. Name three reasons every Christian should witness.

_____

_____

_____

2. List the four major points to emphasize when witnessing and give a Scripture reference for each point.

_____

_____

_____

_____

3. Does praying a prayer automatically make a person a Christian? What is the only thing the Bible teaches is man's part of salvation?_____

_____

4. Once a person has believed on Christ, what are some ways you could help him grow?

_____

_____

Verses to Memorize

- Romans 3:23
- Romans 6:23
- Romans 5:8
- Romans 10:9

7
BAPTISM

Perhaps you have heard of someone getting baptized. Maybe you've even seen someone baptized in the past. But what is baptism? How important is it? Why are people baptized?

In this lesson you will discover that baptism is a significant part of every true believer's life. Let's explore its importance and what it represents.

Baptism Is Important

- Read Luke 3:21, 22. According to these verses, what is the first thing Christ did before He began His public ministry? _____

  _____

- According to Acts 10:48, was baptism requested or commanded by Peter? _____

- Would you say that anything commanded by God's ministers and exemplified by Christ was unimportant?
  ☐ Yes ☐ No

The Purpose of Baptism

It is clear that the Bible teaches the importance of baptism, but what is its purpose?

Baptism Does Not Save

You have seen that baptism is not necessary for salvation because you are saved by grace. Salvation is a free gift from God.

- Read Acts 10:44–48 carefully. Did the people believe and receive the Holy Spirit (that is, were they saved) before or after they were baptized? _____

- Read Acts 8:35–38. What would have hindered the eunuch from being baptized? _____ _____

- Did the eunuch believe before or after baptism? _____

Then What Does Baptism Do?

Baptism Is a Picture

Baptism is a picture of what happens in salvation. When you are baptized, you go through three positions that picture Christ's work and our new position in Him. Note three positions in baptism.

- Standing in the water (Christ's death)
- Placed under the water (Christ's burial)
- Coming up out of the water (Christ's resurrection)

Baptism also pictures three things that happen to the believer because he is in Christ.

1. *He is dead with Christ.* What do Galatians 2:20 and Colossians 3:3 say concerning this?

   _____
   _____

2. *He is buried with Christ.* Read Romans 6:3, 4. What does it mean to be buried with Christ?

   _____
   _____

3. *He is a new creature in Christ, raised with Him to walk in newness of life.* Note Romans 6:4, 5 and Colossians 3:1. What are the responsibilities of resurrected people?

    _____

    _____

- Second Peter 1:4 speaks of a new nature! What kind of nature is it?_____

    _____

- Second Corinthians 5:17 states that if any man is in Christ He is a _____ _____. Old things have passed away, and all things are made new.

- Read Colossians 3:1-17. What are some things that should be passing away in the believer's life?

    _____

    _____

    _____

- What are some new things that a believer will begin to see in their life as they grow in Christ?

    _____

    _____

    _____

If you have not followed the Lord in baptism, you are living in open disobedience to the known command of the Lord! You should have a desire to confess to others in the beautiful picture of baptism what Christ has done for you.

Complete This Section without Looking Back at the Lesson

1. What are two reasons baptism is important?

    _____

    _____

2. How does the story of the Ethiopian eunuch prove a person is not saved by baptism?

_____

_____

_____

3. Name the three positions of baptism and what each pictures in Christ's work.

_____

_____

_____

4. What three things does baptism picture about the believer's life?

_____

_____

_____

Verses to Memorize

- Romans 6:3, 4

8

THE BELIEVER AND
THE CHURCH

Another aspect of your growth as a Christian is attending church regularly. The church was instituted by Christ as the means by which Christians can receive greater training in the things of the Lord.

> ## I Don't Believe in the Church! I Don't See Why We Have It!

The Importance of the Church

Some believers try to serve God outside the institution of the local church. They feel the local church has failed and that they can worship God better by gathering in little Bible study groups. They may mean well, but they are not following the teaching of Christ concerning the church.

Christ Instituted the Church as God's Way to Carry out God's Work

Read Matthew 16:18 and Acts 20:28.

- Who builds the church? _____

- To whom does the church belong? _____

- What did He pay for it? _____

- Will the church fail? ☐ Yes   ☐ No

His Church Will Not Fail

Note again Matthew 16:18. Some churches are not good churches. Some of them do not even believe the Bible! Of course, this kind of church is not of the Lord and is not for you. If you're already a member of this kind of church, leave and see if you can find a good one. Maybe the person who led you to the Lord can direct you to a good church. Make sure you find a church that believes the Bible and lives by it. God's churches still exist. Find one and get involved in it!

The Finances of the Church

When we yield ourselves to Christ as Lord and Savior, we yield our pocketbooks, too. All that we have belongs to God, but He has given us the responsibility to serve Him as a steward (manager) of his property. How we manage His property is a reflection of our gratitude to Him for all He has done for us. Giving back to Him is a demonstration of worship.

Stewardship and Tithing

The two words most often used when discussing the Christian's responsibility in giving are *stewardship* and *tithing*. Both words are found in the Bible.

Definition of Stewardship

The word *steward* or *stewardship* is found some 20 times in the King James Bible. It generally refers to someone who manages another's household. Mostly, *stewardship* refers to faithful management of another person's resources.

How Does This Apply to Giving?

Since believers now belong to Christ, all that we have belongs to Him. Thus, we are to faithfully manage both the spiritual and material possessions God has placed at our disposal. We must be faithful in handling our time, our talents, our tongue, and our money. It all belongs to our Lord, and we will give an account to Him for how we faithfully use it.

- Of what are we supposed to be good stewards according to 1 Peter 4:10? _____

_____

- How are we to be good stewards?_____

_____

Definition of Tithing

The word *tithe* means ten percent. It is found primarily in the Old Testament and means to give ten percent of one's income to the Lord. How did this ten percent figure become familiar to us?

We Live in the Age of Grace, Do We Have to Tithe?

History of Tithing

Read each verse below and fill in the missing name.

- _____ started it (Gen. 14:18–20). This was over 400 years before the law was given. Therefore, tithing was a practice of God's people hundreds of years before the Mosaic law.

- _____ continued it (Gen. 28:20–22). This shows that Abraham's experience wasn't an isolated event before the law was given.

- _____ incorporated it (Lev. 27:30). Finally, after 400 years of tithing, this practice is added to the law.

- _____ affirmed it (Matt. 23:23). Jesus commended men for tithing but also warned that there was more to being faithful to Him that simply giving ten percent to the Temple treasury.

The Church's Method of Giving

Read 2 Corinthians 8:1–12; 9:6-14 and 1 Corinthians 16:1, 2 and state how we are to give according to the following verses.

- 2 Corinthians 8:3, 11, 12_____

- 2 Corinthians 9:7_____

- 2 Corinthians 8:2_____

  These people were in extreme poverty but gave far beyond their means.

- 1 Corinthians 16:1, 2_____

- What phrase in 2 Corinthians 8:12 teaches the same truth? _____

  _____

From these passages, we can see that willing, sacrificial giving was the pattern that Paul encouraged and that the early church demonstrated. How much we give is not nearly as important as the attitude behind our giving.

- On what day was the money given? _____

- Where was the money given? _____

  From there, it was distributed around the world.

- What was the greatest result of their giving (2 Cor. 9:11-13)? _____

Do I Have to Give My Offerings to the Church, or Can I Give to Whomever I Want?

God's institution for conducting His work on earth in this age is the local church. We ought to give our offerings to support our local church first, rather than spread them out and give them as we please to various organizations.

- What phrase in 1 Corinthians 16:2 proves that the money was brought to the church and collected weekly rather than kept by each man in his own house until Paul came? _____

_____

Our giving to the local church today ought to be willing, sacrificial, and proportional to how God has blessed us. Although the books in the New Testament that were written to churches do not command a specific percentage of our income that we ought to give, the fact that Abraham and Jacob willingly gave a tithe is an excellent example of willing, proportional giving. The other question we need to ask ourselves is, "How is my giving sacrificial?" Perhaps a tithe would be very sacrificial, but for some of us it might not be sacrificial at all. How much has Christ sacrificed for us?

- Why would it not be fair for God to set a definite amount that all should give—such as $100 a month?

  _____

  _____

  _____

Does your giving show that you are willing to sacrifice to show Him the gratitude and worship that He deserves? How can your giving better demonstrate that God and His church are more important to you than your possessions?

The Necessity of the Church

- Hebrews 10:25 tells us why we need the church. In your own words, what does it say concerning the necessity of the church?_____

  _____

  _____

Christians Need Fellowship

When you're at school, you're with the unsaved. At work you must rub shoulders with unbelievers. Everywhere you go you must associate with those who don't know the Lord. Therefore, you desperately need a time of fellowship with those who can strengthen you and can talk about the things of the Lord. Read Malachi 3:16.

- What three things did the people in this verse do?

  _____

  _____

  _____

- How did the Lord respond?

  _____

  _____

Christians Need to Be Taught the Word

The early Christians stayed together daily, continuing in the Apostles' doctrine (Acts 2:42). That means they were learning the Word as the Apostles taught them. Acts 6:1-4 shows that the Apostles had two major responsibilities—to pray and to study/ teach the Word of God. For this reason deacons were selected.

- Why did the early church find it necessary to appoint deacons? _____

  _____

Most good churches have a Sunday school or other teaching time for you to attend that will further train you in Bible truths. Also, the morning worship service and other weekly meetings will help you in the things of the Lord. Whenever your church meets, you have an opportunity to learn to know God better through His Word and to fellowship and encourage His people. How does your faithfulness to your church's services reflect a commitment to grow as a believer?

Complete This Section without Looking Back at the Lesson

1. Should a Christian serve the Lord through the church or apart from the church? _____
    Why? _____
    _____

2. Should we leave the institution of the church because some churches have quit teaching the truth?
    ☐ Yes   ☐ No

3. If your church does not teach the truth, what should you do about it? _____

4. What does "tithe" mean? _____
    _____

5. Where is our offering to be given? _____

6. Name two reasons why you need the church.
    _____
    _____

Verses to Memorize
*   Hebrews 10:25
*   1 Peter 4:10

EXAMINATION QUESTIONS

Complete the following questions without looking back in your book for answers.

1. In your own words, state whether or not you are a born again Christian and how you know you are saved.

   _____

   _____

   _____

   _____

   _____

2. How many people have sinned? _____

3. What are the wages for sin? _____

4. What must a person do to be saved? _____

   _____

5. Can unsaved people do anything right and pleasing to God? ☐ Yes ☐ No

6. In God's sight how do man's righteousnesses (his attempts to earn salvation) appear? _____

   _____

7. Write out Ephesians 2:8, 9 from memory.

   _____

   _____

   _____

   _____

   _____

8. What passage in the Bible teaches that you can know you have eternal life? _____

9. What verses teach that you are in Christ's hands?

_____

_____

10. Write out Romans 10:9 from memory.

_____

_____

_____

_____

11. How much of God's Word is true? _____

12. Name five things a study of the Word of God will do in your life.

_____

_____

_____

_____

_____

13. Why was God's Word written? _____

_____

_____

14. List three ways you should treat the Word of God.

_____

_____

_____

15. Write out 2 Timothy 2:15 from memory.

_____

_____

_____

_____

16. What is the secret of Bible study?

_____

_____

_____

17. Summarize the "Story of God's Glory."

_____

_____

_____

_____

_____

_____

18. What are the results of seeing God's glory in the Bible?

_____

_____

19. Who is the only person that can understand God's Word?

_____

Why can he understand it?_____

_____

20. Write out 1 Corinthians 2:14 from memory.

_____

_____

_____

_____

21. What is prayer? _____

_____

22. What one thing hinders prayer? _____

23. To whom, in whose name, and in whose power should
    you pray? _____

_____

_____

24. Write out 1 Timothy 2:8 from memory.

_____

_____

_____

_____

25. Name four reasons every Christian should witness.

_____

_____

_____

_____

26. List the four major points to emphasize when witnessing and give Scripture for each point.

_____

_____

_____

_____

27. What are the two passages of Scripture that are especially good to use in giving a person the assurance of his salvation? _____

_____

28. What are two things you could do to help a new believer to grow? _____

_____

29. Write out Romans 5:8 from memory.

_____

_____

_____

_____

30. Why is a person baptized? _____

_____

_____

31. What are the three positions in baptism, and what do they represent?

_____

_____

_____

32. Should a person serve the Lord through the church or apart from the church?_____
Why? _____

_____

_____

33. Where should you give your offerings?

_____

34. Name two reasons why you need the church.

_____

_____

35. If your church does not preach the truth, what should you do about it?

_____

_____

36. Who owns the church?_____
What did He pay for it?_____

_____

Congratulations on completing the *Milk* booklet! You are well on your way to genuine Christian growth. The next book in our Christian Growth series, *Meat: For Growing Christians*, can be a tool to help you continue your journey. You can order it by calling our toll free number (800-688-3008) or through our website (www.positiveaction.org).